The Book of Ruth

You are holding a reproduction of an original work that is in the public domain in the United States of America, and possibly other countries. You may freely copy and distribute this work as no entity (individual or corporate) has a copyright on the body of the work. This book may contain prior copyright references, and library stamps (as most of these works were scanned from library copies). These have been scanned and retained as part of the historical artifact.

This book may have occasional imperfections such as missing or blurred pages, poor pictures, errant marks, etc. that were either part of the original artifact, or were introduced by the scanning process. We believe this work is culturally important, and despite the imperfections, have elected to bring it back into print as part of our continuing commitment to the preservation of printed works worldwide. We appreciate your understanding of the imperfections in the preservation process, and hope you enjoy this valuable book.

*THE CAMBRIDGE BIBLE
FOR SCHOOLS AND COLLEGES*

THE
BOOK OF RUTH

CAMBRIDGE UNIVERSITY PRESS
C. F. CLAY, Manager

LONDON
FETTER LANE, E.C. 4

EDINBURGH
100 Princes Street

NEW YORK: G. P. PUTNAM'S SONS
BOMBAY, CALCUTTA, MADRAS: MACMILLAN AND CO., Ltd.
TORONTO: J. M. DENT AND SONS, Ltd.
TOKYO: THE MARUZEN-KABUSHIKI-KAISHA

All rights reserved

THE
BOOK OF RUTH

in the Revised Version

with introduction and notes

by

G. A. COOKE, D.D.

Hon. D.D, Edin.; Oriel Professor of the Interpretation of
Holy Scripture, Oxford, and Canon of Rochester;
Hon. Canon of St Mary's Cathedral, Edinburgh

Cambridge:
at the University Press
1918

First Edition 1913.
Reprinted 1918.

PREFACE

BY THE

GENERAL EDITOR FOR THE OLD TESTAMENT

THE present General Editor for the Old Testament in the Cambridge Bible for Schools and Colleges desires to say that, in accordance with the policy of his predecessor the Bishop of Worcester, he does not hold himself responsible for the particular interpretations adopted or for the opinions expressed by the editors of the several Books, nor has he endeavoured to bring them into agreement with one another. It is inevitable that there should be differences of opinion in regard to many questions of criticism and interpretation, and it seems best that these differences should find free expression in different volumes. He has endeavoured to secure, as far as possible, that the general scope and character of the series should be observed, and that views which have a reasonable claim to consideration should not be ignored, but he has felt it best that the final responsibility should, in general, rest with the individual contributors.

A. F. KIRKPATRICK.

CONTENTS

	PAGE
LIST OF PRINCIPAL ABBREVIATIONS	viii
INTRODUCTION:	
§ 1. Contents and aim of the Book	xi
§ 2. Date of the Book	xv
§ 3. Place of the Book in the Canon	xvi
TEXT AND NOTES	1
INDEX	21

LIST OF PRINCIPAL ABBREVIATIONS

Ber. Rab.	The Midrash Rabbah, *Bereshith* (Genesis).
Bertheau	E. Bertheau, *Das Buch der Richter und Ruth*, 2nd edn., 1883.
Budde	K. Budde, *Das Buch der Richter*, 1897, in Marti's Kurzer Hand-Commentar zum Alten Testament.
Buhl	F. Buhl, *Geographie des Alten Palastina*, 1896.
CIS.	*Corpus Inscriptionum Semiticarum.*
COT.[2]	E. Schrader, *The Cuneiform Inscriptions and the Old Testament*, 2nd edn., 1885.
D	Deuteronomy (7th cent. B.C.) and Deuteronomist.
Driver, *Introd.*[8]	S. R. Driver, *An Introduction to the Literature of the Old Testament*, 8th edn., 1909.
Driver, *Schweich Lectures.*	S. R. Driver, *Modern Research as illustrating the Bible*, 1909. The Schweich Lectures for 1908.
E	Elohist, Hexateuchal source, written probably in the Northern Kingdom, 9th–8th cent. B.C.
Encycl. Bibl.	*Encyclopaedia Biblica*, edited by T. K. Cheyne and J. Sutherland Black, 4 vols., 1899–1903.
EV	English Version or Versions (AV. and RV.).
HDB. or *DB.*	Hastings' *Dictionary of the Bible*, 5 vols., 1898–1904.
J	Jehovist, Hexateuchal source, written probably in Judah, 9th cent. B.C.
KAT.[3]	*Die Keilinschriften und das Alte Testament*. 3rd edn., 1903, by H. Zimmern and H. Winckler.
KB.	E. Schrader, *Keilinschriftliche Bibliothek* (transliterations and translations of Babylonian and Assyrian texts, by various scholars), 6 vols., 1889–1900.

LIST OF ABBREVIATIONS

Ḳimḥi	The commentary of David Ḳimḥi of Narbonne (A.D. 1160–1235), printed in Rabbinic Bibles.
Lagrange	M.-J. Lagrange, *Le Livre des Juges*, 1903.
LXX.	The Septuagint in Swete's edition, *The Old Testament in Greek*, vol. i., 1887. (3rd edn., 1901.)
LXX. cod. B LXX. MSS. LXX cod. A	Two Greek versions of Judges exist; the one represented by codex B (Vaticanus) and a considerable group of cursives designated N by Moore; the other represented by codex A (Alexandrinus) and the majority of MSS. both uncial and cursive. Codex B is printed as the text of Swete's edition, with the readings of codex A below; the latter has been edited separately by Brooke and McLean, 1897.
LXX. Luc. LXX. MSS.	Among the cursive MSS. which belong to the version represented by codex A is a group which furnishes the text published by Lagarde, *Librorum Veteris Testamenti Canonicorum pars prior*, 1883, and is thought to give the recension of Lucian. Another set of cursives, belonging also to the version of codex A, forms a second group, designated M by Moore.
Moore	George F. Moore, *A Critical and Exegetical Commentary on Judges*, in the International Critical Commentary series, 1895. Also *Judges* in the Polychrome Bible, English translation and notes, 1898; Hebrew Text and critical notes, 1900.
Nowack	W. Nowack, *Richter und Ruth*, 1900, in Nowack's Handkommentar zum Alten Testament.
NSI.	G. A. Cooke, *A Text-book of North-Semitic Inscriptions*, 1903.
Onom. or *OS.*	Paul de Lagarde, *Onomastica Sacra*, 1870; written in Greek by Eusebius, and translated into Latin by Jerome. This edition is cited by pages and lines.
OTJC.[2]	W. Robertson Smith, *The Old Testament in the Jewish Church*, 2nd edn., 1892.
Pesh. or Syr	Peshitto, the Syriac Version of the Bible.

LIST OF ABBREVIATIONS

Rashi	The commentary of R(abbi) Sh(ĕlōmoh) Y(iṣḥāḳi) of Troyes, A.D. 1040—1105, printed in Rabbinic Bibles.
RD	The Deuteronomic Redactor.
RVm	The Revised Version marginal notes.
Syro-Hex.	The Syriac version, ascribed to Paul of Tella, of the Septuagint column in Origen's Hexapla, representing the Hexaplaric LXX. as it was read at Alexandria in the beginning of the 7th cent. A.D.
Vulg.	Vulgate, Jerome's Latin Version of the Bible.
ZDPV.	*Zeitschrift des Deutschen Palaestina-Vereins.*

A small 'superior' figure attached to the title of a book (e.g. *Introd.*[8]) indicates the *edition* of the work referred to.

In citations, e.g. Jud. ii. 1 b, 5 a, the letters a, b (sometimes c, d) denote respectively the first and second (or third and fourth) parts of the verse cited.

The citations always refer to the English Version; occasionally, where the Hebrew numbering differs from the English, attention is called to the fact.

In the transliteration of Hebrew and Arabic words or proper names the following equivalents are used: $' = $ א; $' = $ ע; $gh = $ غ; $ḥ = $ ח, ح, kh (in Arabic words) $ = $ خ; $dh = $ ذ; $ḳ = $ ק, ق, $ṣ = $ צ, ص; $ṭ = $ ט, ط.

Bertholet's commentary, *Das Buch Ruth* (1898) in Marti's Kurzer Hand-Commentar zum Alten Testament, is referred to by the name of the author.

A German translation of the *Midrash Ruth Rabbah* has been published by A. Wünsche (Leipzig, 1883).

INTRODUCTION

§ 1. Contents and Aim of the Book

THE ancient narratives of the Book of Judges carry us back to a half-barbarous age of struggle and disorder, memorable chiefly for the deeds of Israel's heroes: the Book of Ruth, although the scene is laid in the same age, gives us a very different picture. It introduces us to the peaceful life of the home and of the village, with its sorrows and joys, its wholesome industry and kindly virtues; a life which is by no means barren of heroic qualities, but they take the form of unselfish affection and generosity and loyalty to the ties of kindred; a simple community, tenacious of long established customs, and penetrated throughout by a spirit of unaffected piety. No doubt the picture is idealized; but the author, so far from inventing facts which never existed, is evidently describing a life with which he was familiar. How true to nature are his incidental touches! the excitement of the women-folk over Naomi's return and their interest in the birth of the child, the grave approval of the elders sitting in the gate, the cautious prudence of the 'near kinsman.'

Other parts of the Old Testament create a far less favourable impression of the religion of the people; their superstitions and crude beliefs, even their wilful unfaithfulness which stirred the indignation of the prophets, confront us again and again. But in the later literature, especially in the Wisdom Books and in some of the Psalms, we find plenty of evidence to shew that there must have been many homes in Israel beside those of Naomi and Boaz which were hallowed by the fear of God and love of family, many a village beside Beth-lehem in which an act of disinterested charity would win approval 'in the gate.' For such companion-pictures to Ruth we can point to Job i 1—5, xxiv., Ps. cxxvii., cxxviii., cxxxiii, Prov. xxxi. 10—31, Tobit ii., Judith viii. 1—8, Ecclus. xl. 18—27. The religious homes of which we catch a glimpse at the beginning of the New Testament, homes like those of Elisabeth and Zechariah and of the Holy Family, could trace an ancestry of many generations in ordinary Jewish life.

But the aim of our author was not merely to give an idyllic description of a God-fearing, pastoral community. This forms only the background from which his principal persons stand out: it is their characters, and the events of their lives, which make up the substance of his story. The sorrows of Naomi, which have not deprived her of that rarest of gifts, "a heart at leisure from itself To soothe and sympathize"; the devotion of Ruth, which leads her to forget her own people and her father's house, and fulfil her duty by the family of her dead husband; the generosity of Boaz, shewn by his compassion for the young widow, and then by taking upon himself the redemption of Naomi's property, and, crowning act of all, by his marrying Ruth as part of the kinsman's obligation: these are the author's chief concern, and his way of handling them gives its charm and value to the Book. At the same time the story afforded him an opportunity to bring out certain further points. One was the fact that a Moabite woman, the daughter of an alien race and faith, could be a pattern of the highest virtues, and faithful to the customs of her adopted country (ii. 11, iii. 9 f.). Another was the commendable piety of a next of kin marriage with a childless widow (ch. iv.); not necessarily a levirate marriage (Deut. xxv. 5 ff.), for Boaz was not the *levir* or brother in law of Ruth's dead husband, but a marriage analogous to it in principle and object. Finally, the author intended to shew how by this particular marriage Ruth became the great grandmother of David (iv. 17), a matter of special interest to all Jewish readers.

From what has been said about its contents, it will be manifest that the Book of Ruth cannot be described as history in the sense in which the early narratives of Judges, Samuel, and Kings are history; in the Hebrew Bible it is not classed among the historical books, and it was written long after the time with which it professes to deal. Yet we may feel certain that the story is based upon historical truth; the scene and the characters which fill it are unmistakeably true to life; the author drew upon facts of experience, and at the same time, we may well believe, made use of certain family traditions relating to David[1]. Out of these he wove his tale, which he intended to be "an example to his own age as well as an interesting sketch of the past" (Robertson Smith and Cheyne, *Encycl. Bibl.*, col. 4172).

This, however, is not the view of the author's purpose which is taken by many modern scholars[2]. Ruth is supposed to have been written as a protest against the rigorous measures adopted by Ezra and Nehemiah when they discovered the danger of mixed marriages (Ezr. ix., x., Neh. x. 30, xiii. 23—27). It is true, of course, that the author represents a Moabite woman as a pattern of all that an Israelite wife should be, and tells how she was admitted to a place of honour in an illustrious Hebrew family; but it argues a singular lack of imagination and literary insight to treat the Book of Ruth as a counter-blast or manifesto. "Surely no one who thoroughly appreciates the charm of this book will be satisfied with the prevalent theory of its object. There is no 'tendency' about the book; it represents in no degree a party programme" (*Encycl. Bibl.*, l.c.). Had the author written with any such intention, why did he disguise it so artfully? We may question whether Jewish readers in the time of Nehemiah would have detected a protest against his policy any more readily than we do in such a guileless piece of literature

[1] It has been suggested that some of the traditional elements in the story were drawn from mythology or folk-lore; Winckler, *Altorient. Forschungen*, iii. pp. 66 f., *KAT*.[3], pp. 229, 438. It would be rash to deny the possibility that such was the case, but the evidence alleged is not very convincing.

[2] E.g. Geiger, *Urschrift u. Uebersetzungen*, pp. 49 ff.; Kuenen, *Religion of Isr.*, ii., p. 242 f.; Graetz, *History of the Jews*, i., p. 381 f; Kautzsch, *Lit of O.T*, p. 129 f.; Bertholet, *Comment.*, p. 52 f.; Nowack, *Comment.*, p. 184 f.

§ 2. DATE OF THE BOOK

While it is impossible to accept the Rabbinic tradition that "Samuel wrote his book and Judges and Ruth" (Talm. *Baba Bathra* 14 *b*), modern opinion is not entirely agreed about the date of Ruth; we can only attempt to indicate generally the period to which the Book seems to belong

(*a*) Though the writer professes to deal with the ancient times in which the immediate ancestors of David flourished, and gives to his story a certain archaic colouring, this is only a literary device, like that which lays the scene of Job in the days of the patriarchs. For, as has been said above, the state of society which Ruth describes is very different from the conditions presupposed by the early narratives of Judges. The author looks back upon that rough and stormy age through a twilight of fancy, and in fact the very phrase "when the judges judged" (i. 1) reproduces the view of the period which was formulated by the Deuteronomic editor, and may well imply that the author was acquainted with the Book of Judges, at any rate in its Deuteronomic form. Moreover, the way in which David is brought into the story shews, quite apart from the pedigree in iv. 18—22, that he has become the king of later imagination and legend; the climax is reached when the story arrives at the name of David (iv. 17). Whether any indication of date can be found in the explanation of an old custom given in iv. 7 is not certain, for the verse may be a gloss inserted into the text (see note *in loc.*); on the other hand, the verses before and after do not form a natural sequence without it; and supposing that it comes from the author's hand, we may conclude that in his time the custom, which was well understood in the age of Deuteronomy (Deut xxv. 9 f), needed explanation; the great cleavage in social life caused by the exile had intervened.

(*b*) An examination of the style, i.e. of the idioms and syntax, of the Book seems to point to a comparatively late period. We must admit that the style on the whole is classical, and "palpably different not merely from that of Esther and Chronicles, but even from Nehemiah's memoirs or Jonah":

INTRODUCTION

hence so good a judge as Dr Driver cannot satisfy himself that the Book is as late as the 5th cent. B.C. (*Introd.*[8], p. 454), and considers it to belong to the pre-exilic period. Certainly the writer uses expressions which occur in literature of the classical age, but these may only shew that he was familiar with the Books of Samuel and Kings: e.g.

Jehovah do so to me, and more also i 17; 1 Sam. iii. 17 and ten times in Sam. and Kings.

was moved ('rang again') i. 19; 1 S. iv. 5, 1 K. i. 45.

hap, chance ii. 3; 1 S. vi. 9, xx. 26.

such a one iv. 1; 1 S. xxi. 2, 2 K. vi. 8.

uncover thine ear iv 4; 1 S ix. 15 and six times in Sam.

the seed which Jehovah shall give iv. 12, 1 S. ii. 20.

The older form of the 1st pers. pronoun (אנכי) occurs seven times, the later form (אני) twice.

Again, we find certain grammatical forms which are not decisive as to age, but occur most frequently in later books: e.g.

the impf. 2nd. fem. in ין׳ ii. 8, 21, iii. 4, 18; 1 S. i. 14, Is. xlv. 10, Jer. xxxi. 22.

the perf. 2nd. fem. in תי׳ iii. 3, 4; often in Jer., Ezek. xvi., Mic. iv. 13.

Other forms and expressions distinctly point to a post-exilic date: e.g.

take wives (נשא אשה for the earlier לקח אשה) i. 4; Ezr. ix. 2, 12, Neh. xiii. 25, 1 Chr. xxiii. 22 etc.

therefore (להן) i. 13 is pure Aramaic; Dan ii 6 etc.

tarry, hope (שׂבר) i. 13; Ps. cxix 166, Esth. ix. 1.

stay, be shut up (עגן) i. 13; elsewhere in Jewish Aramaic.

Mara i. 20 has the Aram. fem. ending (מרא = Hebr. מרה).

Almighty (*Shaddai,* not *El Shaddai*) i 20; Num. xxiv. 4, 16, and often in Job.

confirm (קים) iv. 7; Ezek xiii. 6, Esth. ix. 21, 27, 29, 31 f., Ps cxix. 28, 106, Dan. vi. 8 (Aram.).

Thus on the whole the language and style of Ruth appear to indicate that the Book was written after, rather than before, the exile. As we have seen, the author deliberately goes back to early times for the setting of his narrative, and it is in keeping with this that he has adopted certain phrases from the older historical books; but now and again he could not avoid using expressions which reveal the period to which he belonged.

(c) A more promising clue to the date is the fact that Ruth shews no signs of the influence of the Deuteronomic school, which profoundly affected all the historical writings which have come down to us from pre-exilic times; and since the author seems to have known Judges in its Deuteronomic form, we may infer that he lived later than the age of Jeremiah. But it may be questioned whether the period just before the exile, or the early years of the struggling community which built the Second Temple, would have been favourable to the composition of such a work as Ruth, so serene in its outlook and tone of gracious piety. And if we cannot fairly detect in the Book a protest against the policy of Ezra and Nehemiah, there is no reason to suppose that it was contemporary with the latter (432 B.C. is the date of his second visit to Jerusalem). By the time that Chronicles was composed, shortly after 333 B.C., the past history of Israel was interpreted from a peculiar point of view; the legalist temper had become predominant, and Ruth is as free from the rigid spirit of legal orthodoxy as it is from the Deuteronomic pragmatism. At some time, then, in the century following Nehemiah it seems probable that the story was written; and if we are at all near the mark in this conclusion, the Book of Ruth acquires an additional interest, as proving that in an age which was becoming more and more absorbed in the ideals of legalism, the spirit of Hebrew literature was not extinct, but capable of producing a fresh and lovely work, remarkable especially for a large-hearted charity which could welcome, for her goodness, a Moabite woman into a Jewish home; so that the Book, like Jonah, may be called in the words of Dr Cheyne, "a noble record of the catholic tendency of early Judaism."

§ 3. Place of the Book in the Canon

In the Jewish Canon Ruth is placed among the *Kethûbîm* or Hagiographa (Psalms—Chronicles), and in printed Hebrew Bibles follows the Song of Songs as the second of the five *Megillôth* or Rolls, which were read at certain seasons in the synagogue[1]. If Ruth had been known at the time when the historical books, Joshua—Kings, were collected, its account of David's ancestry, a matter of such great interest and not recorded in the older histories, would certainly have secured for it a place among them. Moreover, the historical books have all passed through the process of Deuteronomic redaction, while Ruth differs from them in this respect, and therefore, most probably, was not inserted into the older collection.

In the English Bible, as in the Septuagint and Vulgate, Ruth has been moved from the place which it holds in the Hebrew Bible, and is made to follow the Book of Judges. The reason for this transference is obvious enough; the opening words of Ruth suggested it. Some scholars have even thought that the LXX. and Vulgate have preserved the true order, and that originally Ruth was written as an appendix to Judges; for only by counting Judges and Ruth as one[2], and Jeremiah and Lamentations as one, can the books of the Old Testament be made to number 22, according to the reckoning of Josephus (*contra Apionem* i. 8; so Origen, Epiphanius, Jerome). This argument, however, cannot bear much weight when we find that Jewish tradition gives the total as 24 (Apocalypse of Ezra xiv. 44—46, Talm. *Baba B.* 14 *b*, 15 *a*): indeed the number is counted in various ways. Finally, it is easy to see why Ruth was placed after Judges in the Greek and Latin Bibles; but we cannot account for its position among the Hagiographa if that was not its original place in the Canon, and no hint of any other place has reached us from Jewish tradition.

[1] Song of Songs at Passover; Ruth at Pentecost; Lamentations on the 9th of Ab (the day of the destruction of Jerusalem); Koheleth at Tabernacles; Esther at Purim. The arrangement of the five Megilloth is due to post-Talmudic liturgical usage. According to the Talmudic order (*Baba Bathra* 14 *b*), which is probably the most ancient, Ruth comes before the Psalms, the genealogy of David before his writings. See Ryle, *Canon of the O.T.*, pp. 232 ff., 281 f.

[2] So Jerome (*Prol. Gal.*), in agreement with Origen and Melito of Sardes: (Hebraei) in eumdem (librum Judicum) compingunt Ruth.

THE BOOK OF RUTH

AND it came to pass in the days when the judges judged, 1
that there was a famine in the land. And a certain man of
Beth-lehem-judah went to sojourn in the ¹country of Moab,
he, and his wife, and his two sons. And the name of the 2
man was Elimelech, and the name of his wife ²Naomi, and

¹ Heb. *field.*   ² Heb. *Noomi.*

Ch. i. *Ruth's devotion: she leaves her home and follows
Naomi to Judah.*

1. *in the days when the judges judged*] The scene of the following
story is thus placed in a distant age, which the writer pictures as a time
of idyllic peace. Evidently the Book of Judges was known to him. the
opening phrase is based upon the Dtc. editor's theory set forth in
Jud. ii. 16 ff. For *judges* as a title see Introd. to Judges, p. xi.

a famine in the land] Targ. *the land of Israel*; more probably, the
land in which Beth-lehem was situated. In ancient times it was only
strong necessity which induced people to leave their homes, cf 2 Kings
viii. 1; for a foreign country meant a foreign religion (*v.* 16), 'How
shall we sing Jehovah's song in a strange land?' See Am. vii. 17,
Hos. ix. 3.

to sojourn] as a protected alien; cf. Jud. xvii. 7 *n.*

the country of Moab] lit. *the field of M.*, similarly in *vv.* 2, 6, 22, ii. 6,
iv. 3; cf. *the field of the Philistines* 1 Sam. xxvii. 5, 7. Moab lay on
the E. of the Jordan.

2. *Elimelech*] i e. *God,* or *my God, is king*; an ancient name in
S. Palestine, occurring in the Amarna tablets, Ilu-milki 179, 36; 151, 45,
though the form *Milk-ilu-* is commoner; in Phoenician we find the
corresponding *Baal-milk* = 'Baal is king,' *NSI.*, p. 347. *Naomi* on
the surface appears to mean *my sweetness,* a name like Hephzi-bah
(2 Kings xxi. 1) expressive of the mother's joy in the new-born child;
more likely it is an Aram. fem. form of *Naamān,* i.e. *sweet, pleasant one,*
which gives a clear parallel to Marah = *bitter one* in *v.* 20; Wellhausen
compares the Aram. names Ohorān and Oharî, and the Arab. Nu'mân
and Nu'mâ, *Composition d. Hex.*², p. 358 *n.* The meaning of *Mahlon*

the name of his two sons Mahlon and Chilion, Ephrathites of Beth-lehem-judah. And they came into the country 3 of Moab, and continued there. And Elimelech Naomi's 4 husband died; and she was left, and her two sons. And they took them wives of the women of Moab; the name of the one was Orpah, and the name of the other Ruth: and 5 they dwelled there about ten years. And Mahlon and Chilion died both of them; and the woman was left of her 6 two children and of her husband. Then she arose with her daughters in law, that she might return from the country of Moab: for she had heard in the country of Moab how that the LORD had visited his people in giving them bread. 7 And she went forth out of the place where she was, and her two daughters in law with her; and they went on the way 8 to return unto the land of Judah. And Naomi said unto her two daughters in law, Go, return each of you to her mother's house: the LORD deal kindly with you, as ye have

and *Chilion* is not quite certain; if it is *weakening* and *pining* the names may have been chosen for their significance.

Ephrathites]'Apparently Ephrath was the name of the district round Beth-lehem; cf. 1 Sam. xvii. 12, and see Gen. xxxv. 19, Mic. v. 2, Ps. cxxxii. 6.

4. *took them wives*] The idiom is a late one, 2 Chr. xi. 21, Ezr. ix. 2, 12, Neh. xiii. 25 etc.; see Introd. p. xv. It is uncertain whether the names of the two wives have any bearing upon the parts which they play in the story. The Midrash Rabbah on this Book explains that *Orpah* was so called 'because she turned her *neck* ('*oreph*) on her mother in law'; possibly the name may = 'obstinacy' (cf *stiffnecked*, Ex. xxxii. 9 etc.). Equally doubtful is the significance of *Ruth*; if the name is shortened from *re'uth*, as it is written in Syriac, it will be the fem. of *Re'u* (Gen. xi. 18 ff.), and may mean 'friendship.' We cannot, therefore, feel sure that the writer invented the names; he may have derived them from tradition.

6. *the LORD had visited his people*] i.e. shewn a practical interest in; cf. Gen. l. 24 f. E, Ex. iii. 16, iv. 31 J; St Lk. i. 68, vii. 16. Apparently the famine lasted ten years, *v.* 4. With *giving them bread* cf. Ps. cxxxii. 15.

7. *to return*] Strictly only appropriate to Naomi, cf. i 22 etc.; the author unconsciously reveals that he is writing from Palestine.

8. *to her mother's house*] although Ruth's father was alive, ii. 11; but the natural place for the female members of the family would be their mother's tent or house, cf. Gen. xxiv. 28, 67, Song iii. 4.

the LORD deal kindly with you, as ye have dealt] Cf. Ps. xviii. 25 'with the kind thou shewest thyself kind.' Jehovah's *kindness* was

dealt with the dead, and with me. The LORD grant you 9
that ye may find rest, each of you in the house of her husband.
Then she kissed them; and they lifted up their voice, and
wept. And they said unto her, Nay, but we will return 10
with thee unto thy people. And Naomi said, Turn again, 11
my daughters: why will ye go with me? have I yet sons in
my womb, that they may be your husbands? Turn again, 12
my daughters, go your way; for I am too old to have an
husband. If I should say, I have hope, if I should even have
an husband to-night, and should also bear sons; would ye 13
therefore tarry till they were grown? would ye therefore stay

specially needed by the widow, for her condition was regarded as a reproach, Is. iv. 1, liv. 4. The Book of the Covenant makes no provision for the widow (Ex. xxii 22 is a later expansion); contrast the humanity of Deut. xxiv. 19—21, xxvii. 19.

On her marriage the wife united herself to her husband's religion; when she returned to her own people as a widow, she returned to their religion if they were foreigners, *v.* 15 f. Yet Jehovah's influence is not entirely confined to the land of Israel; Naomi can commend her daughters in law to His protection when they were back in their own land.

9. *that ye may find rest*] Cf. iii. 1; Naomi had in her mind another home for them, i.e. a second marriage. The story is told with much naturalness and delicacy.

11. *have I yet sons. that they may be your husbands?*] Alluding to the custom of levirate marriage, i.e. marriage with a brother in law (Lat. *levir*) after the husband's death. The law on the subject is given in Deut. xxv. 5—10; cf. St Mt. xxii. 24.

12. *I am too old to have an husband*] Naomi does not seriously contemplate any application of the custom alluded to: not only has she no surviving sons, but she never can have any.

If I should say etc.] Strictly, 'that I should have said, I have hope' (scil. of children). For the grammar cf. Gen. xl. 15 ('that they should have put me'), 1 Sam. xvii. 26 b.

13. *would ye therefore tarry till they were grown?*] The narrative in Gen. xxxviii. shews that the custom of levirate marriage was presupposed for the patriarchal age, but in a more primitive form than that of the modified law in Deut. xxv. According to Gen. xxxviii. a son, though not of marriageable age, is bound by a positive requirement of the divine will to marry his brother's widow, and she must remain a widow *till he be grown up* (ib. *v.* 11). The identity of the latter expression with that in the present verse seems to imply a reminiscence of the patriarchal narrative. But Naomi's imaginary sons, the offspring of an impossible second marriage, would be half-brothers to Mahlon and Chilion; and there is nothing to shew that a levirate marriage was customary in such a case. Moreover, the object of this kind of marriage

4   RUTH I. 13—16

from having husbands? nay, my daughters; for ¹it grieveth me much for your sakes, for the hand of the LORD is gone 14 forth against me. And they lifted up their voice, and wept again: and Orpah kissed her mother in law; but Ruth 15 clave unto her. And she said, Behold, thy sister in law is gone back unto her people, and unto her god: return thou 16 after thy sister in law. And Ruth said, Intreat me not to leave thee, and to return from following after thee: for whither thou goest, I will go; and where thou lodgest, I will lodge: thy people shall be my people, and thy God

¹ Or, *it is far more bitter for me than for you*

was to prevent the extinction of a family and the transference of the family property into the hands of strangers. As a matter of fact, however, Naomi is not thinking of this at all; she is not lamenting that her sons died without children, but that Ruth and Orpah have lost their husbands; her one anxiety is for the future welfare of her daughters in law. Hence, though her language is coloured by a reference to a well-known social institution, the reference is not exact, nor intended to be taken literally.

It is noticeable that several words in this verse point to the post-exilic date of the writer: *therefore* is represented by a pure Aramaic word, Dan. ii. 6, 9, iv. 27 [Aram. 24]; *tarry*, again in Esth. ix. 1, Ps. cxix. 166 ('hoped'); *stay*, lit. *be restrained, shut up*, only here in the O.T.; in Aramaic the pass. ptcp. is used of a wife *tied* to a husband and deserted and *prohibited* from marrying again, e.g. Talm. Jerus. *Gittin* iv. 45 c.

it grieveth me much for your sakes] lit. *it is very bitter for me because of you*; for this use of the prep. (*min*=*because of*) cf. Eccl. ii. 10, Ps. xxxi. 11, cvii. 17 etc. Naomi's sympathy goes out to the young widows, and she urges them to seek happiness elsewhere. The rendering in the marg. means, 'You can go back and marry again; a worse lot is in store for me, I must remain a solitary.' The rendering of the text is to be preferred as more in accordance with Naomi's unselfish feeling.

14. *Orpah kissed her mother in law*] and, it is implied, said good-bye.

15. *unto her people, and unto her god*] i.e. Chemosh, the god of the Moabites, Num. xxi. 29, 1 Kings xi. 33. The ancient belief here receives its simplest expression: each land and people had its own Deity inseparably connected with it; outside lay the territory of another god. The Israelites, at any rate the popular religion in Israel, did not deny the divinity of the gods of the neighbouring lands, though for themselves Jehovah was the only God; cf. Jud. xi. 24, 1 Sam. xxvi. 19. So when Orpah goes back to Moab she goes back to her native god; similarly, when Ruth determines to make her home in Judah, she declares her intention of adopting the religion of her new country, *v*. 16. See *v*. 8 *n*.

my God: where thou diest, will I die, and there will I be 17 buried: the LORD do so to me, and more also, if aught but death part thee and me. And when she saw that she was 18 stedfastly minded to go with her, she left speaking unto her. So they two went until they came to Beth-lehem. 19 And it came to pass, when they were come to Beth-lehem, that all the city was moved about them, and *the women* said, Is this Naomi? And she said unto them, Call me not 20 ¹Naomi, call me ²Mara: for the Almighty hath dealt very bitterly with me. I went out full, and the LORD hath 21 brought me home again empty: why call ye me Naomi, seeing the LORD hath testified against me, and the Almighty

¹ That is, *Pleasant*.   ² That is, *Bitter*.

17. *will I die ..be buried*] According to ancient thought union in life meant union in death and in the grave; the members of a family had a common burying-place, Gen. xlvii. 30, xlix. 29. In the underworld they lived together, as families and by nations; cf. the expression 'he was gathered to his people,' i.e. his fellow-tribesmen, and see Ezek. xxxii. 17—32.

the LORD do so to me, and more also] Jehovah has already become the God of Ruth, and she uses the name of Israel's God in a solemn imprecation, which occurs only here and in the books of Samuel and Kings. When heathen utter this oath, *Elohim* is used instead of Jehovah, and the verbs are plural, 1 K. xix. 2, xx. 10. Lit. the phrase here runs 'Jehovah do so to me, and more also—(only) death shall separate me from thee'; the substance of the oath is an assertion, not a negation; similarly 1 Sam. xiv. 44, xx. 13, 1 K. ii. 23 etc. in the Hebr.

19. *all the city was moved*] *was in a stir*; so 1 Sam. iv. 5, 1 K. i. 45 ('rang again'). Beth-lehem was a small place; Naomi's return without her husband and sons could not escape notice; it aroused keen excitement, especially among the women—a graphic touch, true to life.

20. *Mara*] The word has the Aramaic, not the Hebr. fem. ending.

the Almighty hath dealt very bitterly with me] Almost the same words as in Job xxvii. 2. For *Almighty* the Heb. has *Shaddai*, perhaps an intentional archaism, see Gen. xlix. 25. Shaddai alone (not El Shaddai) occurs elsewhere only in poetry, e.g. Num. xxiv. 4, 16 and in Job; Naomi's words in *v*. 21 fall into poetic rhythm, as the language of emotion usually does in the O.T.

21. *hath testified against me*] i.e. hath marked His displeasure by the misfortunes which have overtaken me; for the idiom cf. Num. xxxv. 30, 1 Sam. xii. 3. The Targ. characteristically moralizes: it was on account of Naomi's sin (in migrating to a heathen country). The LXX. and Vulg., pronouncing the verb differently, render *hath humbled me*, but against the Hebr. construction. Underlying the words is the

22 hath afflicted me? So Naomi returned, and Ruth the Moabitess, her daughter in law, with her, which returned out of the country of Moab: and they came to Beth-lehem in the beginning of barley harvest.

2 And Naomi had a kinsman of her husband's, a mighty man of ¹wealth, of the family of Elimelech; and his name 2 was Boaz. And Ruth the Moabitess said unto Naomi, Let me now go to the field, and glean among the ears of corn after him in whose sight I shall find grace. And she said 3 unto her, Go, my daughter. And she went, and came and gleaned in the field after the reapers: and her hap was to light on the portion of the field belonging unto Boaz, who 4 was of the family of Elimelech. And, behold, Boaz came from Beth-lehem, and said unto the reapers, The LORD be

¹ Or, *valour*

conviction, so deeply rooted in the Hebrew mind, that all must go well with the righteous and that misfortune was a sign of Jehovah's wrath.

22. *which returned out of the country of Moab*] A superfluous expression after *Naomi returned*, and possibly an insertion from n. 6, unless we regard it as a standing description of Ruth.

in the beginning of barley harvest] i.e. in April. Barley was the first crop to be cut, Ex. ix. 31 f., 2 Sam. xxi. 9.

Ch. ii. *The generosity of Boaz: his first meeting with Ruth.*

1. *a kinsman*] Strictly the word does not mean more than *familiar friend* 2 Kings x. 11, Prov. vii. 4.

a mighty man of wealth] **a wealthy man**, 1 Sam. ix. 1, 2 Kings xv. 20; sometimes the phrase means *a valiant man* (marg.) Jud. vi. 12, xi. 1; in iii. 11 the word for *wealth* has a moral sense.

Boaz] Cf. 1 Kings vii. 21. The derivation of the name is uncertain: possibly, 'in him is strength' (for Ruth). More probably the name is traditional, and a contraction of Ba‘al-‘az i.e. 'B. is strong'; cf. in Phoenician *Bomilcar* for Ba‘al-melkarth, *Salambo* for Salm-ba‘al etc.

2. Permission to glean in the harvest field was allowed to the poor, the stranger, the fatherless, and the widow; naturally it depended on the goodwill of the owner; see Deut. xxiv. 19, Lev. xix. 9 f., xxiii. 22.

3. *her hap...Boaz*] The word for *hap* occurs in 1 Sam. vi. 9 ('a chance'), xx. 26. Throughout the story the writer intends us to share his strong belief in Providence, over-ruling unpremeditated actions and words (cf. *vv.* 12, 19 f.), and rewarding those who trust it (iii. 4, 9, 11, iv. 6, 14). 'The cosmos is a fighter for the righteous,' says the Jewish sage, Wisd. xvi. 17.

with you. And they answered him, The LORD bless thee. Then said Boaz unto his servant that was set over the 5 reapers, Whose damsel is this? And the servant that was 6 set over the reapers answered and said, It is the Moabitish damsel that came back with Naomi out of the country of Moab: and she said, Let me glean, I pray you, and gather 7 after the reapers among the sheaves: so she came, and hath continued even from the morning until now, save that she tarried a little in the house. Then said Boaz unto Ruth, 8 Hearest thou not, my daughter? Go not to glean in another field, neither pass from hence, but abide here fast by my maidens. Let thine eyes be on the field that they do reap, 9 and go thou after them: have I not charged the young men that they shall not touch thee? and when thou art athirst, go unto the vessels, and drink of that which the young men have drawn. Then she fell on her face, and bowed herself 10 to the ground, and said unto him, Why have I found grace in thy sight, that thou shouldest take knowledge of me, seeing I am a stranger? And Boaz answered and said 11 unto her, It hath fully been shewed me, all that thou hast done unto thy mother in law since the death of thine

4. *The LORD be with you*] Cf. Jud vi. 12, Ps. cxxix. 8. A religious spirit governs the relations between employer and employed on this estate.

7. *save that she tarried a little in the house*] lit. 'her dwelling in the house is (but) short': not *the house* of Boaz, which is out of the question; possibly *her own house*, in which case the meaning will be 'she has but recently come to live here.' It is doubtful, however, whether the words can bear this sense; the text is probably corrupt. The LXX. reads 'and she hath not rested in the field (even) a little time', the Vulg., 'and not even for a moment hath she returned to the house.' Something can be said for each of these emendations, but neither is quite satisfactory.

9. *after them*] i.e. the maidens v. 8, who followed the reapers and did the binding.

10. *take knowledge of me*] with kindly purpose, *v.* 19, Ps. cxlii. 4. A stranger had no right or claims on protection in a foreign land. The Hebr. has a subtle play on the two words *take knowledge of me* and *stranger*; the roots are distinct, but they sound alike.

11. Ruth's uncommon devotion, which induced her to leave her native land and the natural guardians of her widowhood, is one of the main features of the story.

husband: and how thou hast left thy father and thy mother, and the land of thy nativity, and art come unto a people 12 which thou knewest not heretofore. The LORD recompense thy work, and a full reward be given thee of the LORD, the God of Israel, under whose wings thou art come to take 13 refuge. Then she said, Let me find grace in thy sight, my lord; for that thou hast comforted me, and for that thou hast spoken [1]kindly unto thine handmaid, though I be not 14 as one of thine handmaidens. And at meal-time Boaz said unto her, Come hither, and eat of the bread, and dip thy morsel in the vinegar. And she sat beside the reapers: and [2]they reached her parched corn, and she did eat, and was suf-15 ficed, and left thereof. And when she was risen up to glean, Boaz commanded his young men, saying, Let her glean even 16 among the sheaves, and reproach her not. And also pull out some for her from the bundles, and leave it, and let her 17 glean, and rebuke her not. So she gleaned in the field until even; and she beat out that she had gleaned, and it was 18 about an ephah of barley. And she took it up, and went into the city: and her mother in law saw what she had gleaned: and she brought forth and gave to her that she

[1] Heb. *to the heart of.*   [2] Or, *he*

12. *the LORD recompense*] Cf. i. 8.

under whose wings ..refuge] This beautiful idea is repeated in Ps. xxxvi. 7, lvii. 2, xci. 4; the figure is that of an eagle, Deut. xxxii. 11. May the God of Israel take care of the homeless stranger from a heathen country! The prayer was answered through the agency of him who uttered it—a fine touch, as Bertholet points out.

13. *comforted . spoken kindly unto*] The same words in Is. xl. 1, 2. See on Jud. xix. 3.

though I be not] As a stranger Ruth is not like one of his handmaidens; she has no right to expect such friendly treatment.

14. *in the vinegar*] i.e. sour wine. It is said to be still used in Palestine by the harvesters as a relish with bread.

parched corn] i.e. grain taken from the newly reaped corn and roasted in a pan, and eaten with bread or as a substitute for bread.

16. *the bundles*] Only here; in Assyr. the root (*ṣabâtu*) means 'to grasp'; in the Mishnah and Jewish Aram., 'to bind.'

17. *she beat out*] Cf. Jud. vi. 11.

an ephah] Approximately equivalent to our bushel.

18. *her mother in law saw*] A slight change of pronunciation gives a more expressive sense: *she shewed her mother in law*.

had left after she was sufficed. And her mother in law said 19
unto her, Where hast thou gleaned to-day? and where
wroughtest thou? blessed be he that did take knowledge of
thee. And she shewed her mother in law with whom she
had wrought, and said, The man's name with whom I
wrought to-day is Boaz. And Naomi said unto her daughter 20
in law, Blessed be he of the LORD, who hath not left off his
kindness to the living and to the dead. And Naomi said
unto her, The man is nigh of kin unto us, ¹one of our near
kinsmen. And Ruth the Moabitess said, Yea, he said unto 21
me, Thou shalt keep fast by my young men, until they have
ended all my harvest. And Naomi said unto Ruth her 22
daughter in law, It is good, my daughter, that thou go out
with his maidens, and that they meet thee not in any other
field. So she kept fast by the maidens of Boaz to glean 23
unto the end of barley harvest and of wheat harvest; and
she dwelt with her mother in law.

And Naomi her mother in law said unto her, My daughter, 3
shall I not seek ²rest for thee, that it may be well with
thee? And now is there not Boaz our kinsman, with whose 2

¹ Or, *one of them that hath the right to redeem for us* See Lev. xxv. 25.
² Or, *a resting place*

19. *blessed be he*] Naomi invokes a blessing on the benefactor before
she knows who he is; the author delights in such dramatic fitness, cf.
v. 12, iii. 11.
20. *one of our near kinsmen*] See marg. and note on iii. 9. Here
the word *go'el* occurs for the first time in the story.
22. *in any other field*] In the field of a less pious man than Boaz
a poor maiden might come to mischief; cf. v. 9.
23. *wheat harvest*] followed two or three weeks later.
she dwelt with] Or, with a slight change, *she returned unto*; so
Vulg.

Ch. iii. *Ruth appeals to Boaz to do the kinsman's part.*

1. *seek rest*] a resting place marg.; see on i. 9. All arrangements
for a marriage were made by the parents (cf. Jud. xiv. 2 f.); hence it
was Naomi's duty to provide for Ruth's future. How this was done is
told with fine simplicity.
2. *our kinsman*] See on ii. 1, a different word from *near kinsman*
(*go'el*) in v. 9. His relationship to Elimelech, and the friendly disposition
which he had shewn, led Naomi to think of Boaz in considering 'a

maidens thou wast? Behold, he winnoweth barley to-night
3 in the threshing-floor. Wash thyself therefore, and anoint
thee, and put thy raiment upon thee, and get thee down
to the threshing-floor: but make not thyself known unto
the man, until he shall have done eating and drinking.
4 And it shall be, when he lieth down, that thou shalt mark
the place where he shall lie, and thou shalt go in, and
uncover his feet, and lay thee down; and he will tell thee
5 what thou shalt do. And she said unto her, All that thou
6 [1]sayest I will do. And she went down unto the threshing-
floor, and did according to all that her mother in law bade
7 her. And when Boaz had eaten and drunk, and his heart
was merry, he went to lie down at the end of the heap of
corn: and she came softly, and uncovered his feet, and
8 laid her down. And it came to pass at midnight, that the
man was [2]afraid, and turned himself: and, behold, a woman
9 lay at his feet. And he said, Who art thou? And she
answered, I am Ruth thine handmaid: spread therefore thy

---

[1] Another reading is, *sayest unto me*.   [2] Or, *startled*

resting place' for Ruth. He might be willing to do the kinsman's
part; at any rate, she made up her mind to act courageously and in a
spirit of faith. In her plan for a next of kin marriage Naomi's only
concern is for Ruth's future, the perpetuation of the name of her dead
childless son is left for Boaz to mention (iv. 5, 10).

to-night] when the wind blows (Targ.), and the weather is cool. In
Palestine a wind rises from the sea at about four o'clock in the afternoon,
and lasts till half an hour before sunset. For *the threshing-floor* an
exposed, open spot was chosen on the side or summit of a hill; here it
must have lain outside the village, and to reach it Ruth had to *go down*
the hills on which Beth-lehem stands.

3. *Wash thyself...and anoint thee, and put thy raiment upon thee*] as
a bride prepares herself for marriage; see Ezek. xvi. 9 ff.

4. *And it shall be*] More accurately, *and let it be that thou mark*;
cf. 1 Sam. x. 5, 2 Sam. v. 24 in Hebr.

his feet] lit. *the place of his feet*, where they were covered against the
cold of night. Outside this chapter the word occurs only in Dan. x. 6;
cf. 1 Sam. xix. 13 etc., lit. *the place of his head*.

7. *at the end of the heap of corn*] To this day peasants are ac-
customed to sleep on the threshing-floor in the open air.

8. *and turned himself*] A reflexive form of the verb, which means
'to grasp with a twisting motion'; the verb occurs again only in
Jud. xvi. 29 ('took hold of'), Job vi. 18 ('are turned aside' mg.).

skirt over thine handmaid; for thou art ¹a near kinsman.
And he said, Blessed be thou of the LORD, my daughter: 10
thou hast shewed more kindness in the latter end than at
the beginning, inasmuch as thou followedst not young men,
whether poor or rich. And now, my daughter, fear not; 11
I will do to thee all that thou sayest: for all the ²city of my

¹ Or, *one that hath the right to redeem* Heb. *goel*.
² Heb. *gate*. See ch. iv. 1, 11.

9. *spread therefore thy skirt over thy handmaid*] This symbolic act denoted that the kinsman claimed the widow as his wife. Cf. Ezek. xvi. 8. The custom prevailed among the early Arabs; a good illustration is given in Tabari's commentary on the Koran (Sura iv. 23, forbidding men to 'inherit women against their will'): 'In the Jâhilîya, when a man's father or brother or son died and left a widow, the dead man's heir, if he came at once and threw his garment over her, had the right to marry her under the dowry of [i.e. already paid by] her [deceased] lord, or to give her in marriage and take her dowry. But if she anticipated him and went off to her own people, then the disposal of her hand belonged to herself'; Robertson Smith, *Kinship* etc., p. 87. See also Sale's translation of the Koran (Warne & Co.), p. 56 and note.

a near kinsman] The primary meaning of the Hebr. *go'el* is 'one who enforces a claim' which has lapsed, so 'one who re-claims' or 're-vindicates.' Hence the verb is used of *redeeming* a house or field after it has been sold, or an Israelite who has been obliged to sell himself as a slave (Lev. xxv. 25 ff., 47 ff.), or something which has been vowed to Jehovah; in the expression *go'el had-dām*, 'the avenger of blood,' Deut. xix. 6, 12 etc., it denotes 'one who vindicates the rights of the murdered man;' see Driver in loc. But since a man was not as a rule able himself to *redeem* a right which had lapsed, the duty fell upon his family and more particularly upon his nearest relative; in this way *go'el* came to mean 'the next of kin.' Boaz, however, was not the nearest relative (v. 12), so he could not act unless the next of kin declined; nor did the Pentateuchal law require the *go'el* to marry the widow of the deceased in addition to redeeming his property, though custom sanctioned the marriage. Hence Ruth's appeal to the generosity of Boaz.

10. *thou hast shewed more kindness*] At the outset Ruth had shewn her piety towards her mother in law (ii. 11); now she shews it towards her husband's family. She has declined to seek a second marriage outside, and by her action the dead will come by his rights.

11. *I will do to thee all that thou sayest*] Note v. 4 'he will tell thee what thou shalt do'; but Ruth herself suggested what Boaz was to tell. The coincidence was guided by Jehovah's good providence.

all the city, lit. *gate*] In ancient times the gate was a place of resort for conversation and business and the administration of justice; cf. iv. 1, 11, Gen. xxiii. 10, xxxiv. 20, Job xxix. 7, Prov. xxxi. 23.

12 people doth know that thou art a virtuous woman. And now it is true that I am a near kinsman: howbeit there is
13 a kinsman nearer than I. Tarry this night, and it shall be in the morning, that if he will perform unto thee the part of a kinsman, well; let him do the kinsman's part: but if he will not do the part of a kinsman to thee, then will I do the part of a kinsman to thee, as the Lord liveth: lie down
14 until the morning. And she lay at his feet until the morning: and she rose up before one could discern another. For he said, Let it not be known that the woman came to the
15 threshing-floor. And he said, Bring the mantle that is upon thee, and hold it; and she held it: and he measured six *measures* of barley, and laid it on her: and [1]he went into
16 the city. And when she came to her mother in law, she said, [2]Who art thou, my daughter? And she told her all
17 that the man had done to her. And she said, These six *measures* of barley gave he me; for he [3]said, Go not empty

[1] Or, according to some ancient authorities, *she went*
[2] Or, *How hast thou fared*   [3] Another reading is, *said to me*.

a virtuous woman] See ii. 1 *n*. and Prov. xxxi. 10. There was no unbecoming forwardness in Ruth's conduct; it is to be judged in accordance with the customs of the time.

12. *there is a kinsman nearer than I*] with a better right to do the kinsman's part. Boaz displays a nice sense of honour, and a desire to adhere strictly to the rules of social usage.

13. *Tarry this night*] as a precaution against chance perils; see Song v. 7.

14. *For he said*] i.e. to himself, *he thought*; 'if I should say' in i. 12 has the same meaning. His thought shewed consideration and good sense.

15. *the mantle*] Only again in Is. iii. 22; apparently a large wrap worn over the ordinary clothes.

six measures *of barley*] The measure to be supplied is uncertain: six *seahs*=two ephahs (i.e. bushels), which the Targ. gives, or six *ephahs*, would be too heavy to carry; hence it is suggested that six *omers* are meant = ⅗ of an ephah, Ex xvi. 36. The gift is intended for Naomi, who would have to consent to the marriage, as standing in the relation of parent to Ruth. Mr S. A. Cook points out a parallel in a Babylonian tablet (*KB*. iv. p. 187, xi. lines 1—6), where the widowed mother is approached by the intending bridegroom; *The Laws of Moses and the Code of Hammurabi*, p 75 *n*.

16 *Who art thou*] i.e. *how art thou? how hast thou fared?* Cf. Gen. xxvii. 18.

unto thy mother in law. Then said she, Sit still, my daughter, 18 until thou know how the matter will fall: for the man will not rest, until he have finished the thing this day.

Now Boaz went up to the gate, and sat him down there: and, behold, the [1]near kinsman of whom Boaz spake came by; unto whom he said, Ho, such a one! turn aside, sit down here. And he turned aside, and sat down. And he 2 took ten men of the elders of the city, and said, Sit ye down here. And they sat down. And he said unto the near 3 kinsman, Naomi, that is come again out of the country of Moab, selleth the parcel of land, which was our brother Elimelech's: and I thought to [2]disclose it unto thee, saying, 4 Buy it before them that sit here, and before the elders of

[1] See ch. ii. 20.   [2] Heb. *uncover thine ear*.

Ch. iv. *Ruth's marriage and descendants.*

1. *Now Boaz went up*] He had decided to redeem Elimelech's estate if the next of kin refused the obligation; this is the primary meaning of the transaction about to be described. *went up*, i.e. from the threshing-floor; cf. *go down* iii. 3, of the opposite direction. Bethlehem is situated on the summit of two knolls.

the gate] where family law was administered, Deut. xxv. 7; cf. iii. 11 *n*. Boaz knew that the Go'el would be passing out of the town in the morning.

Ho, such a one!] A form of address indicating a definite person without expressly naming him; cf. 1 Sam. xxi. 2, 2 K. vi. 8 (of a place).

2. *the elders*] possessed magisterial authority, and could be summoned to deal not only with criminal charges (Deut. xix. 12, xxi. 2—4, 1 K. xxi. 8 ff.), but with cases affecting the rights of a family (Deut. xxv. 7—9).

3. *selleth*] The tense is perfect, and implies *is resolved to sell*; the sale does not take place till *v.* 9. Cf. Gen. xxiii. 11, 13, for the same idiomatic use of the perfect. Naomi came into possession of her husband's property after his death, see *v.* 9 *n.*; this was not in accordance with Pentateuchal law, which says nothing about the inheritance of widows.

our brother] in the wider sense of member of a family or race; cf. Ex. ii. 11, Lev. xix. 17, Jud. xiv. 3 etc.

4. *disclose it*] See marg.; lit. the phrase means to draw aside the long hair covering the ear in order to whisper something, cf. 1 Sam. ix. 15, xx. 2 and elsewhere in Samuel.

them that sit here] appear to be *all the people* of *vv.* 9, 11, as distinct from *the elders*.

my people. If thou wilt redeem it, redeem it: but if ¹thou wilt not redeem it, then tell me, that I may know: for there is none to redeem it beside thee; and I am after thee.
5 And he said, I will redeem it. Then said Boaz, What day thou buyest the field of the hand of Naomi, thou must buy it also of Ruth the Moabitess, the wife of the dead, to raise

¹ So many ancient authorities. The printed Hebrew text has, *he will*.

If thou wilt redeem it, redeem it] It was for the Go'el to decide whether he would buy the land or allow it to pass out of the family; Lev. xxv. 25. A parallel case occurs in Jer. xxxii. 7—9: Jeremiah's cousin, wishing to sell some family property, offers it first to the prophet as next of kin; the prophet exercises his right and buys in the estate.

but if thou wilt not redeem it] See marg.; a slight correction required by the context.

5. *thou must buy it also of Ruth*] The text is certainly wrong, for it gives a misleading sense; with a small change read as in *v.* 10, **Ruth also thou must buy**, with Vulg., Pesh.; the LXX. gives both translations! Rendered strictly the whole sentence runs 'What day thou buyest...thou wilt have bought (perf.) Ruth also'; see Driver, *Tenses*, § 124.

In primitive and semi-primitive societies women have no independent rights of their own; they are treated as part of the property of the family to which they belong. Hence 'a wife who had been brought into her husband's house by contract and payment of a price to her father was not free by the death of her husband to marry again at will. The right to her hand lay with the nearest heir of the dead' (Robertson Smith, *Encycl. Bibl.*, col. 4166). This was the old law in Arabia to the time of Mohammed, and that it prevailed with some modifications among the ancient Hebrews is shewn by the narrative in Gen. xxxviii. (see on i. 13 above), by the law of levirate marriage in Deut. xxv. 5 ff., and by the present story, which implies that for the nearest kinsman to marry the widow was regarded as an act of compassion. It is important to notice that the law of Deut. xxv. 5 ff. applies only to the case of brothers living together on the same estate; if one dies without a son, the survivor is bound to marry the widow. But neither the Go'el here, nor Boaz, was a brother of Ruth's late husband; this, therefore, was not a levirate marriage. Again, in the Pentateuch (Lev. xxv.) the Go'el is not required to purchase the widow as well as the land of the dead kinsman, and it is clear that in the present case the Go'el did not consider that he was under an obligation to do so; he agrees to purchase the land (*v.* 4), but when he is told that this involves the purchase of Ruth, he withdraws his consent. At the same time we gather from his language in *v.* 6, and from the applause of the people in the gate, that custom admitted the propriety of the double purchase. It was in fact a work of charity, going beyond the

up the name of the dead upon his inheritance. And the near 6
kinsman said, I cannot redeem it for myself, lest I mar mine
own inheritance · take thou my right of redemption on thee;
for I cannot redeem it. Now this was *the custom* in former 7
time in Israel concerning redeeming and concerning exchanging, for to confirm all things; a man drew off his shoe,
and gave it to his neighbour: and this was the *manner of* attestation in Israel. So the near kinsman said unto Boaz, Buy it 8
for thyself. And he drew off his shoe. And Boaz said unto 9

strict letter of the law but sanctioned by ancient usage, and thoroughly in keeping with the generous, kindly disposition of Boaz. The writer holds him up as an edifying example.

to raise up the name of the dead] Again the law of levirate marriage furnishes a parallel; the object of such a marriage was 'to raise up unto his brother a name in Israel' Deut. xxv. 7, as well as to prevent the estate passing out of the family. To leave behind no name in the community was considered a grave misfortune (cf. *v.* 10); it meant that the dead was deprived of the reverence and service of posterity (cf. 2 Sam. xviii. 18). This feeling may be traced back to the religious instinct which prompted the worship of ancestors.

6. *lest I mar mine own inheritance*] When the Go'el learns that if he redeems the estate he is expected to marry the widow, he takes back his promise (*v.* 4). He declares that he cannot afford to be so generous. If he were to have a son by Ruth, the child would take the name and estate of the dead, and the Go'el would have only a temporary usufruct in the property, and in the end lose it altogether (Robertson Smith l.c.).

take thou my right of redemption on thee] Since the Go'el declines, the right to redeem falls on Boaz as the next nearest kinsman.

7. *in former time in Israel*] Cf. 1 Sam. ix. 9, which begins similarly. Driver (*Introd.*[8], p. 455) thinks that the present verse is also an explanatory gloss, because it is not needed in the narrative, and has the appearance of being a later addition; see, however, the Introduction, p. xiv.

a man drew off his shoe, and gave it to his neighbour] This old custom was not altogether intelligible in the writer's day, so he gives an explanation of it. When *property was transferred*, as in the present case, to take off the sandal and hand it to the person in whose favour the transfer is made, gave a symbolic attestation to the act and invested it with legal validity (Driver, *Deut.*, p. 283). The same symbolism was used on other occasions, and with varying significance. Thus, when a deceased husband's brother declined to contract a levirate marriage, the widow loosed his sandal from off his foot in token that he *renounced his right* to make her his wife, Deut. xxv. 9; cf. the Arabic form of divorce, 'she was my slipper and I have cast her off' (Robertson Smith, *Kinship* etc., p. 269); the action implied at the same time a feeling

the elders, and unto all the people, Ye are witnesses this day, that I have bought all that was Elimelech's, and all that was 10 Chilion's and Mahlon's, of the hand of Naomi. Moreover Ruth the Moabitess, the wife of Mahlon, have I purchased to be my wife, to raise up the name of the dead upon his inheritance, that the name of the dead be not cut off from among his brethren, and from the gate of his place: ye are 11 witnesses this day. And all the people that were in the gate, and the elders, said, We are witnesses. The LORD make the woman that is come into thine house like Rachel

of contempt, which is probably denoted by the expression in Ps. lx. 8, cviii. 9[1]. The drawing off of the sandal also symbolized among the later Arabs the *renunciation of an oath of fealty* to a sovereign: his authority was withdrawn as the sandal from the foot (Goldziher, *Abhandl. z. Arab. Philologie*, i. p. 47)

9. *Ye are witnesses*] Cf. *v.* 11. With this appeal for confirmation cf. Josh. xxiv. 22, 1 Sam. xii. 5.

I have bought...of the hand of Naomi] More idiomatically the Hebr. perf. should be rendered in English I **buy**, i.e. I stipulate to buy; cf. the perf. in *v.* 3 *selleth*. The purchase-money was to go to Naomi; she had inherited all the family property; even Mahlon's and Chilion's land had passed to their mother, not to their widows, probably because the latter were foreigners. The right of a widow to any share in her husband's estate is not recognized in the Pentateuch[2]; but later practice allowed provision to be made (Judith viii. 7), and permitted the husband to insert a clause in the marriage settlement giving his widow the right to dwell in his house after him, and to be nourished from his wealth all the days of her widowhood; Talm. *Kethuboth* iv. 8.

10. *Moreover Ruth . have I purchased*] do I buy, the same word and tense as in *v.* 9. This was an additional and voluntary feature of the transaction, due to the goodwill of Boaz, and as such receives the applause and congratulations of the people.

to raise up the name of the dead] One object of the marriage was to secure the preservation of the name of the dead (see on *v.* 5); by a legal fiction the child of the marriage would be regarded as the son of Mahlon, *v.* 17 ('a son born to Naomi').

11. *like Rachel and like Leah*] Gen. xxix. 31—xxx. 24. May

[1] Cf. the story told by Burton, *Land of Midian*, ii. p. 196 f.: a man who owned 2000 date-palms was asked by the leader of a band of robbers to sell them; and when he suggested that an offer should be made, the robber, taking off his sandal, exclaimed 'with this!' For the Jewish practice of *Chalitzah*, i.e 'removal' of the shoe, see Oesterley and Box, *Rel and Worship of the Synagogue* (1907), p 294 f.

[2] Contrast the provision of the ancient Babylonian Code: the widow is entitled to her marriage-portion and the settlement which her husband had secured to her in writing, and is allowed to live in his dwelling place, §§ 171 and 150. In this, as in other respects, the Code of Hammurabi represents a more developed civilization than the Pentateuchal law.

and like Leah, which two did build the house of Israel:
and ¹do thou worthily in Ephrathah, and be famous in Bethlehem: and let thy house be like the house of Perez, whom 12
Tamar bare unto Judah, of the seed which the LORD shall
give thee of this young woman. So Boaz took Ruth, and 13
she became his wife; and he went in unto her, and the
LORD gave her conception, and she bare a son. And the 14
women said unto Naomi, Blessed be the LORD, which hath
not left thee this day without a near kinsman, and let his name
be famous in Israel. And he shall be unto thee a restorer 15
of life, and a nourisher of thine old age: for thy daughter
in law, which loveth thee, which is better to thee than seven
sons, hath borne him. And Naomi took the child, and laid 16
it in her bosom, and became nurse unto it. And the 17

¹ Or, *get thee wealth* or *power*

Ruth become the ancestress of a famous race! Dante ranks her fourth after Sarah, Rebecca, Judith, in Paradise; *Parad.* xxxii. 10 ff. For *did build the house of Israel* cf. Deut. xxv. 9 and Gen. xvi. 2, xxx. 3 mg.

do thou worthily] lit. 'achieve might'; the phrase is sometimes rendered 'do valiantly,' e.g. Num. xxiv. 18, Ps. lx. 12, cxviii. 15 f.; but here it is used in a moral sense, cf. iii. 11. The reference is to Boaz, here and in the next sentence.

and be famous] To obtain this meaning the Hebr. text (lit. 'proclaim thou a name') must be slightly altered to 'and let thy name be proclaimed,' cf. v. 14. The LXX. favours this correction. How the wish was fulfilled is shewn in v. 17.

12. *Perez*] is mentioned because he was one of the ancestors of the house of Judah, Gen. xxxviii. 29, and, according to the genealogies, Boaz was his descendant, 1 Chr. ii. 4, 9—11.

the seed which the LORD shall give] Cf. 1 Sam. ii. 20.

14. On account of the words *this day*, Bertholet and Nowack take the *near kinsman* (*go'el*) as referring to the new-born son. It is true that the words which follow, 'let his name be famous,' apply to the child; but throughout the story the *near kinsman* is Boaz. He has done all, and more than all, that could be expected of a *go'el*; he has redeemed the property, and now (*this day*) he has secured an heir for Naomi's family.

15. *better to thee than seven sons*] Ruth has proved it by her piety towards the dead and the living. *Seven* is a round number, cf. 1 Sam. i. 8.

16. *took the child, and laid it in her bosom*] to shew that she adopted the child of Ruth as her own; cf. the phrase 'born upon the knees' Gen. xxx. 3, l. 23.

18 RUTH IV. 17—20

women her neighbours gave it a name, saying, There is
a son born to Naomi; and they called his name Obed:
18 he is the father of [1] Jesse, the father of David.
19 Now these are the generations of Perez: Perez begat
Hezron; and Hezron begat Ram, and Ram begat Am-
20 minadab; and Amminadab begat Nahshon, and Nahshon

[1] Heb. *Ishai.*

17. *the women her neighbours*]. Cf. *v.* 14 and i. 19. In St Lk. i. 58 f. the neighbours and kinsfolk propose to name the child.

There is a son born to Naomi] The child is popularly considered to belong to Naomi's family. Cf. Gen. xxx 3, where the son of Bilhah, born on the knees of Rachel, is regarded as Rachel's child.

Obed] An abbreviated form of Obad-iah 'servant of Jah,' or of Abdi-el 'servant of El.'

the father of Jesse, the father of David] The ancestry of Jesse is not given in 1 Sam. The name (*Ishai*) is perhaps a shortened form of *Abishai.* The story of Ruth thus shews how a Moabite woman obtained an honourable place in the annals of Hebrew history; the rule laid down in Deut. xxiii. 3 [Hebr. 4] had at least one noteworthy exception[1]. From 1 Sam. xxii. 3, 4 we learn that friendly relations existed between David and the Moabites: it may not be fanciful to suppose that he would be all the more ready to entrust his parents to the care of the Moabite king because his father's grandmother was a Moabite.

With this account of the memorable issue of Ruth's marriage the Book is brought to a suitable close. The genealogy which follows may be regarded as a later addition.

18. *these are the generations...begat*] Standing formulae of P, e.g. Gen. v 3—32, vi. 9 ff., x. 1, xi. 10 ff. etc. Though cast into P's form, the genealogy is constructed out of ancient materials. It is attached to Perez, because he is named in *v.* 12.

19 *Hezron begat Ram*] The genealogy occurs with fuller details in 1 Chr. ii. 4—15; according to *ib. vv.* 25, 27 Ram is the son of Jerahmeel and grandson of Hezron. In *ib.* iv. 1 Hezron like Perez is a son of Judah.

Amminadab] i.e. *my kinsman*, or *paternal uncle* (*ammi*), *is generous*, a proper name of an ancient type; see Gray, *Hebr. Prop. Names*, p. 44.

20. *Nahshon*] i e. *serpent*, a name belonging to the early period. This Nahshon son of Amminadab was a prince of Judah (Num. i. 7, ii. 3, x. 14) and a contemporary of Moses and Aaron (Ex. vi. 23), according to P; here he is made the grandfather of Boaz, obviously by omitting a good many links.

[1] The Rabbis get over the difficulty by supposing that the law of Deut. xxiii. 3 applies only to men. Talm *Jebamoth* 76 b; Sifre on Deut. l.c.

begat ¹Salmon; and Salmon begat Boaz, and Boaz begat 21
Obed; and Obed begat Jesse, and Jesse begat David.   22

¹ Heb. *Salmah*.

Salmon]   From Salmah (1 Chr. ii. 11 *Salma*') or Salmon (St Mt. i. 4 f., St Lk. iii. 32) to Boaz is a long step, if the former is the same as 'Salma the father of Beth-lehem' 1 Chr. ii. 51. In St Mt. i. 5 Salmon's wife was Rahab, obviously an anachronism.

22. *and Jesse begat David*] The present genealogy was therefore designed to supply what 1 Sam. omitted, and to trace David's descent from Perez.

Note on the genealogy in vv. 18—22. The following points are to be noticed: (1) The genealogy consists of ten members, of which the first five, from Perez to Nahshon, cover the period from the entry of the Hebrew tribes into Egypt (Perez, Gen. xlvi. 12) to the time of Moses (Nahshon, Num. i. 7); while the last five belong to the period of the settlement in Canaan. It is obvious that the generations are not sufficient to cover this extent of time; the grandfather of Boaz cannot have been a contemporary of Moses. The genealogy, therefore, does not attempt to give a complete historical series; many links are omitted; it is artificially constructed out of traditional materials. (2) The object of the list is to connect David with the princely line of Judah. In spite of his Moabite great-grandmother, he could be shewn to come of the best Judaean stock. How this was done is explained by Wellhausen (*De Gentibus et Familiis Judaeis*, pp. 13—19) as follows: the ancestors of David were known as far as Boaz, but there memory failed; accordingly, as Beth-lehem was the native town of Jesse, it was natural to introduce Salma, 'the father of Beth-lehem' (1 Chr. ii. 51, 54); then David must be connected with the leading family of Judah which flourished in the time of Moses, and, through the marriage of Aaron, united itself with the priestly dignity (Ex. vi. 23). This accounts for Nahshon and Amminadab; these again are traced to Ram, son or grandson of Hezron, whose very name (*Ram* = 'the high one') suggests the founder of a princely line. (3) The date at which the genealogy was drawn up Wellhausen further shews to be post-exilic. For Salma is described in 1 Chr. ii. 51 as a son of Caleb, and the Calebites in ancient times belonged to the S. of Judah (Jud. i. 20); it was not until after the exile, when they found the Edomites in possession of their original seats, that they moved northwards to Beth-lehem and its neighbourhood; so that it was not until after the exile that Salma could be called 'the father of Beth-lehem.' David, however, is never connected with the Calebite district in the S. of Judah, but with the older part of Israel settled in Northern Judah, near the border of Benjamin. (4) The genealogy cannot have been framed by the author of Ruth, because he recognizes Obed as legally the son of Mahlon (iv. 5, 10); if he had drawn up the line himself he would have traced it through Mahlon and Elimelech. We may conclude, therefore, that the genealogy 'forms no integral part of the Book, and may have been added long after the Book itself was written in an age that was devoted to the study of pedigrees' (Driver, *Introd.*[8], pp. 455 f.). (5) The relation between this genealogy and the fuller one in 1 Chr. ii. 10—17 cannot be determined with certainty; for, as Wellhausen has shewn (l.c.), 1 Chr. ii. 10—17, 18—24 is a secondary element, and the same source from which the Chronicler derived 1 Chr. ii. 18—24 may have contained *vv.* 10—17, and it is quite possible that Ruth iv. 18—22 was also derived from it (Nowack). It is simplest to conclude, with Robertson Smith and Cheyne in *Encycl. Bibl.*, that a later writer borrowed the genealogy from 1 Chr. ii. as it stands.

INDEX

adoption, 17
Almighty (*Shaddai*), xv, 5
Arab customs and illustrations, 11, 14, 15

barley harvest, 6
Beth-lehem, xi, 5, 10, 13, 19
Boaz, xii, 6; his estate, 7, 9, 11; decides to redeem, 13 f.; does the kinsman's part, 16; genealogy of, 19 f.
bridegroom's present, 12
burying-place, 5

Caleb, Calebites, 19
Canon, place of Ruth in the, xvi f.
characters in the Book, xii
Chilion, 2 f.
Code of Hammurabi, 16
confirm, xv

Dante, 17
Date of Ruth, xiv–xvi
David, ancestry of, xii, xiv, 18, 19 f.
Deuteronomic editor of Judges, xiv, xvi, 1

elders, 13
Elimelech, 1, 9, 13
ephah, 8, 12
Ephrath, 2

foreign country and religion, 1, 3, 7 f.

gate of the city, 11, 14
genealogy of David, 19 f.
go'el, see kinsman

Hagiographa, xvi f.
Hammurabi, Code of, 16
homes of Israel, xii

Jehovah, God of Israel, 5; His *kindness*, 2 f.; protection, 8; providence, 6, 8, 9, 17
Jerome, xvii
Jesse, 18
judges, 1

kinsman (*familiar friend*), 6, 9 f. (*near k.*, *go'el*), 11, 14, 15, 17
Koran on marriage of widows, 11

language and style of Ruth, xv f.
levirate marriage, xii, 3 f., 14, 15

Mahlon, 1 f., 3, 16, 19
Mara, xv, 5
marriage with next of kin, xii, 10, 11, 14; see levirate marriage
measures, dry, 12
Megilloth, the, xvi f.
Midrash Rabbah (Ruth), 2
migration, 1
Moab, 1, 4, 6, 18 f.

name of the dead, 15
Naomi, xii, 1, 4, 9 f., 13, 16, 18

INDEX

Obed, 18 f.
Orpah, 2, 4

Perez, 17, 19
property, rights of, 11, 14, 15

redemption of property, xii, 11, 13, 14
religion, popular, xii
religious ideas, characteristic, 1, 3, 4
Ruth, her character, xii, 4, 5, 7, 15; name, 2; appeal to Boaz, 11, 12; purchase of, 16; marriage, 17
Ruth, Book of, compared with Judges, xi; in what sense historical, xii f.; traditional elements in, xiii; date, xiv–xvi; peculiarities of language, xv; place in Canon, xvi f.

Salmon, 19
shoe, drawing off, xiv, 15 f.
skirt, spreading of, 11

Talm. Bab., *Baba Bathra*, xiv, xvii; *Kethuboth*, 16; Jer., *Gittin*, 4
therefore (Aramaic), xv, 4
threshing-floor, 10

vinegar, 8

wheat harvest, 9
widows, 2 f.; marriage of, 11, 14; property of, 13, 16; children of, 16, 18
Wisdom Books, xi f.
wives, take, xv, 2
women in primitive society, 11, 14

CPSIA information can be obtained
at www.ICGtesting.com
Printed in the USA
LVOW09*1623200618
581327LV00016BA/386/P

9 781341 180712